Successful Startup
How to use Big Data Marketing to make it big

Fernando C. Gaspar

Carcavelos, Agosto 2018

Fernando C. Gaspar

Dedicated to Tomás

DATASHEET
Title: Successful Startup – How to use Big Data Marketing to make it big
Author: Fernando C. Gaspar
1st edition – Carcavelos, August 2018
ISBN: 9781718014718
fernando.gaspar@apredin.com.pt
www.fernando-gaspar.com

Sophia and Lara, young women with a doctorate in medical sciences and in engineering of materials, respectively, had developed an extremely innovative product able to save many months in recovery of increasingly common fractures of the hip (femur). Both young and highly qualified, speaking excellent English, expressed their dismay and surprise, because the product they had developed was not only the ultimate in terms of technology, but also economically very advantageous, because it would allow savings of millions to insurers and national health services. A needle in a material the human body did not reject (in 99% of cases), allowed the broken bone to stay immobilized and allowed the consolidation in just a little over half the time. "How is it possible that no one has purchased a product with this advantages? From a medical point of view it is very advanced and allows fantastic results, from an economic point of view it can save millions, however, nobody wants to buy. How is it possible? "said Sophia.

"I think it's because Greece has the fame it currently has" said Lara (in 2012), with the heavy appearance of someone who had aged more from this experience than the other 30 years of her life.

It was not easy to explain them that the excellence of the product is not in itself a guarantee of success.

The percentage of startups that fail and close after a few years or just months of activity is frighteningly high. Many studies indicate values above 80%. Even startups created in "protected environments", such as incubators or accelerators, still have very high failure levels. Depending on the studies, between 40 and 60%.

However, these startups are usually created with huge expectations justified by the use of the most advanced technologies to create products and / or services that serve the customers much better.

Using the latest technologies to create better products and services should be a path to success, especially as it should add value to customers' lives, but that does not seem to be the case for many of these startups.

One of the main causes for startup failure is in the marketing strategy adopted.

In more recent times, with the widespread adoption of the "Lean" philosophy in the creation of startups, we have even tried to test with real customers the use of these more advanced technologies to create products that consumers really want.

Brilliant idea, brilliant strategy, create new products customers really want. And yet…

Even with these brilliant strategies, startups continue to fail with a frightening frequency, which justifies studying the reasons behind this failure.

In this book, the main reasons that lead to this failure will be exposed and the radically different actions that can lead a startup to success will be explored.

The most important thing you can gain from reading this short book is learning how to use 21st century marketing technologies.

Content

1.	Reasons for Startups to Fail	6
2.	The typical startup marketing strategy	8
3.	What incumbents do	10
4.	How can startups succeed?	12
	4.1. Storytelling	16
	4.2. Create consumption habits	19
	4.3. Psychometrics	24
	4.4. Big Data Marketing	25
	4.5. Microtargeted communication	26
5.	Conclusions	29
6.	Bio note	32

Objetives

Analyze why startups fail so often
Study the possible role of marketing in preventing these failures
Identify twenty-first century marketing tools and strategies that can help startups

1. Reasons for Startups to Fail

Startups fail for a number of reasons[1], of which stand out:

- Lack of funding;

- Lack of sales.

Far more often, startups fail at selling rather than fail for lack of funding. In fact, lack of funding seems to work as a "filter" that prevents projects that in principle might not be so good to get started, while lack of sales leads to the precipice projects that had already started and looked promising.

But then, why won't these startups sell, when the products and / or services they have developed have convinced the most astute investors and often use the latest technology to improve the lives of customers? The reasons for not selling may be several but they always fall into these areas:

- Lack if notoriety;

- Lack of traction;

- They are beaten by competition.

---

[1] Silva, Francisco M. (2013) *Fatores que contribuem para o insucesso das Startups: O reverso da "medalha"*. Master dissertation at Universidade do Minho, Portugal

Although they offer the most advanced technology (often developed by the startup itself) and have the "best" product for the customer, the truth is that many startups go unnoticed by the target consumer who never gets to know this new offer.

Other startups are successful at getting the target customers' awareness, but then the customers do not adhere to the new product, they do not show interest after they know it, even after trying it.

In one way or another, what happens to startups is that they are beaten by competitors, more often by the incumbent competitors that the consumer has known for a long time, with whose products the consumer has developed long term consumer habits.

As we will observe in more detail, what usually happens is the startup enters the market with the best product, using the best technology, but is beaten by far superior marketing strategies and technologies.

So superior that they remind me of a race between a Ferrari (incumbent) and a bike (startup).

Much of this stems from startups using the latest technology in the development of their product / service, but using nineteenth-century marketing technology.

This is so much the case with the Portuguese startups, as Brazilian or (like in the previous example) Greek!

Let's start by looking at what startups typically do.

2. The typical startup marketing strategy

João and Frederico developed a business idea in support of local commerce during their college years. They want to organize a platform that allows the marketer to attract customers to their offline business online.

Of course they did market research! Focus groups with potential clients, structured interviews with merchants, online surveys to hundreds of potential clients...

"Our prototype received the best reactions from both merchants and customers," said John, tapping his fingers nervously on the table. Neither he nor Frederico understood the difficulty in getting the support they wanted. What could fail?

Typically, when a startup starts it has previously done some sort of market study and has adopted some form of segmentation. You are expected to know which segment you want to sell to.

To convince consumers of this target segment, the startup marketing strategy defines a desired positioning, the image that is intended to build for the brand, usually based on one of the benefits that the product / service intends to provide customers.

Then, to put these ideas into practice, the startup builds a marketing plan, defining, planning and even budgeting what it intends to do to build that image it has defined for its brand, in terms of product, price, place and (generally, especially) of promotion.

Nothing wrong with this line of action. That's what marketing manuals say. For decades they've been saying it.

That really is the problem. For decades incumbent companies have done this. They have already studied the market, have already segmented the market, have already launched brands with incessant advertising messages to occupy the mind of the consumer.

What novelties do the startups bring to this field? As a rule, they try to do the same as the incumbents, with less budget, less notoriety, less experience,...

They may even have better products / services, but the marketing strategy and the marketing technology are the same as always.

> That is, they use marketing technology that was very advanced in the nineteenth century!

> Bicycles

The Lean Startup philosophy has, nevertheless, brought something new. Many startups are nowadays created using advanced marketing strategies.

Following the original work of Steve Blank, they start by trying to find out who are the potential customers and what they really want to buy, then try to validate a replicable sales model, in the phase called customer validation, then look for customers, gaining scale and only in a fourth stage do they establish the normal structure and procedures of a company.

Discovering the customers and what they really want to buy is a much more advanced way of defining the company's offering.

However, when startups get to the stage of building a sales model and replicating it, to gain scale, they are limited to the same strategies and technologies that have been used for decades by the incumbents.

In fact, even in the customer discovery phase startups' efforts are largely focused on identifying the needs of the customers that the startup can satisfy well and defining the target segment to choose from.

In fact, very advanced strategies, but based on the same technology that the incumbents have used for decades.

It's as if the startup competes with a very light carbon-fiber bike with ultra-fast tires. A fantastic bike, super light and fast but ... a bike! (the competition drives a Ferrari, as we will see later).

> That is, marketing technology of the nineteenth century, with 21st century strategies

> Bicycle of the 21st Century

3. What incumbents do

What do you mean, the incumbent competitors drive a Ferrari? What do the incumbent competitors do so different, so advanced?

We should not generalize, so we must focus on the most advanced incumbent competitors, usually large multinationals with large marketing budgets and a long experience in the market.

And what do these companies do?

Many of these companies have already realized that people do not consume to "satisfy needs," nor to "satisfy desires." People consume out of habit.

Man is an animal of habits!

This beaten phrase sums up the essentials of the markets these days. More than 90% of our purchasing decisions are replacement of a product that has ended or somehow repeat a previous decision.

The human being needs routines to feel safe. All our buying behavior aims to establish routines, habits (even if we always say that we hate routine and complain about "boredom"). Just watch the behavior of small children. Whenever my 3 year old arrives late at daycare, the world seems horrible to him, he gets irritable and unstable, instead of being the lovely little creature he always is in the days in which his little routines are respected.

Habits have become the real raw material of marketing.

> Francisco buys shirts at the mall store closest to his house since ... he does not even remember. He purchases food and hygiene and cleaning products in the hypermarket two kilometers from home, ever since it opened.
>
> "Every Saturday I go to dinner at the Brazilian restaurant and every Sunday morning I go to the central cafe to read the newspaper and have coffee."
>
> "Why? It's the habit! "
>
> Francisco does not analyze the alternatives in detail before making each of these purchasing decisions. They are part of his routines, his lifestyle.
>
> "What can make me change? I don't know".

From the marketing point of view, theory taught in the books says "studying markets to meet unmet needs" has long since been useless because there are no longer "unmet needs."

People already satisfy their needs in some way, so they already buy something to satisfy the need we are addressing.

If they are to buy our product / service they will stop buying another, that is, they will change their habits (in this case, consumption habits) and this is something very difficult to achieve!

In fact, the market segments we study turn out to be the result of consumption habits consumers have developed over time.

What can lead people to change their habits? Not much.

They can get fed up with the current habits and look for some variety. Often this means that they will buy a red skirt ... after they have bought a blue one the year before ... and yet they still buy skirts...

Otherwise, they can be convinced that they can improve their lives by changing their habits, despite the great costs that this change always entails.

Or they may be reaching the market and will seek to form new habits.

Given this, what do the incumbents that is so advanced?

- Create habits of consumption, using what psychology teaches us in this respect;

- Reinforce the habits your clients have developed, trying to prevent them from changing;

- Use storytelling to pass on "innocent" and hidden messages to consumers, showing them how they can improve their lives by changing their eating habits or by reinforcing current ones;

- Continuously test the consumer's feelings about the brand.

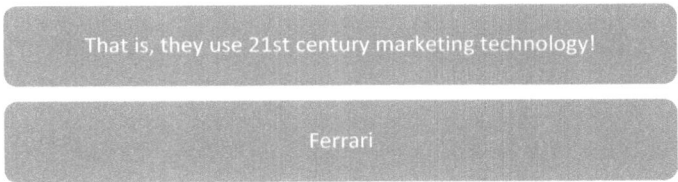

In comparison to startups, they use much more advanced marketing technologies, although using less current product technologies. They drive a Ferrari!

4. How can startups succeed?

We've been looking at what can go badly for startups from a marketing standpoint, but the perspective of this book is not catastrophic, it's upbeat, in large part because these new marketing technologies are easily copied and all marketing is going through a time of great transformation, opening up possibilities for startups not only to keep up with the progress of many incumbents but to go beyond what most brands do today.

First of all, it is necessary that the creation of a startup and / or the launching of a new brand should be focused on the consumption habits of the people and no longer on the segmentation of the market or the needs of these people.

Of course, the consumer needs and their satisfaction continue to be the basis of everything. It is clear that the differences between people's preferences continue to justify differential treatment of different segments. None of this has changed.

What has to change is the focus of the creator of new products or startups.

Continuing to study people's needs will not lead us to discover better ways to satisfy them. Everything is well studied. Even if that happens, it is not by finding a better way to meet the needs of people that they will prefer the new product or startup and change their consumption habits. The story is full of top products that have failed. Does anyone still remember Betamax?

There is no point in continuing to look for the new "miracle" way of segmenting the market. Already tried everything.

The focus of the creation of a new product / service should be the creation of new consumption habits and / or the change of the current habits, to lead the consumer to adopt the new product / service, leaving what he buys.

It is easier to achieve this if the new product / service is higher than the incumbents, but that alone is not enough.

So how can the entrepreneur create or change consumer habits that people have developed over the years to get them to adopt their new product / service?

1. Adopting the knowledge that psychology makes available to us about the creation of habits in the human mind;

2. Using Storytelling to show the consumer that they can improve their story;

3. Using a psychographic segmentation that marketing has known for a long time but until recently it did not have data to apply and that today was made possible thanks to the "sea of data" that we all started to produce;

4. Making use of the latest techniques that we will call for convenience "Big Data" to bring to the consumer a micro segmented communication[2].

Success in introducing a new product implies, in essence:

- Changes in consumption habits;

- Integration into the consumer's lifestyle;

- Integration into the internal narrative of the consumer.

That is, it is necessary to be able to change the consumption habits of the people, so that they integrate the new product / service in their lifestyle.

---

[2] Therefore, we will use the segments that we all already know and studied and we will microsegment with psychometric variables, that is, something that is still little done and can be an advantage for those who enter the market.

For this to happen, we need to get the consumer to integrate into their internal narrative a rationalization of choice for the new product / service.

Internal narrative of the consumer?

What is it?

Psychology teaches us that we all tell little stories of ourselves (and sometimes we share them with others) about our lives.

These stories (narratives) serve for our minds to rationalize, explain, and accept the decisions we have made.

Of course, each person has several narratives in parallel for different areas of their life, but in order to sleep at night it is necessary for our minds to be able to rationalize the decisions we have made in internally acceptable narratives. The most extreme example I know of is about Hitler. He did not say to himself, "I am a horrible monster because today I had millions of Jews murdered." He would certainly have rationalized the decisions he made in narratives acceptable to his mind, of the sort "I am saving the Aryan homeland from the destruction that the Jews were preparing" in order to sleep at night. Still, I find it hard to see how I could sleep, but the capacity of the human mind to rationalize seemingly inexplicable decisions does not cease to amaze me.

Therefore, the ultimate goal of marketing should be how to achieve the (absolutely innocent) ideas in the internal narrative of the consumer, leading him to think that it was he who chose to buy that product / service.

Incredible how this is light years away from the traditional marketing strategy of startups.

Much could be analyzed here on this phenomenon of Rationalization, but we will restrict ourselves to some fundamental points:

- Our tendencies lead to a mental process known as rationalization through which we change our attitudes and beliefs to be able to adapt psychologically;

- Rationalization helps us to give reasons to explain our behavior, even when these reasons may have been drawn by others.

> Our mental process of rationalizing our choices translates into the internal narrative of each

Some of the most important features of this process are:

- We irrationally overestimate our efforts;
    - This leads us, for example, to always thinking that what occupies us time and work is worth more than what really happens. People always overvalue Ikea furniture, after spending a whole Sunday assembling them;
- We always strive to be consistent with our past behaviors;
    - We hate being caught up in contradictions, which means that after something happens the first time

(breaking the ice) it is much easier to make it repeat itself;

- We seek to avoid cognitive dissonance.
    - That unpleasant feeling that we have made a "wrong" choice because it clashes with our beliefs or feelings. We do not like that. Therefore, in Aesop's fable, the fox that tried to catch the grapes when it gave up did not say to itself "they were too high" or "I jump too little." This would disagree with his belief in his own abilities. So the fox said "they were green". We, too, who do not live in an Aesop fable, in our process of rationalizing the decisions we make in life we construct narratives (stories / fables) that help us avoid cognitive dissonance, even if we resort to irrational manipulation of the way we see the world (in the example above, for Hitler it was always the fault of the Jews).

In essence, our choices are the result of this process of rationalization:

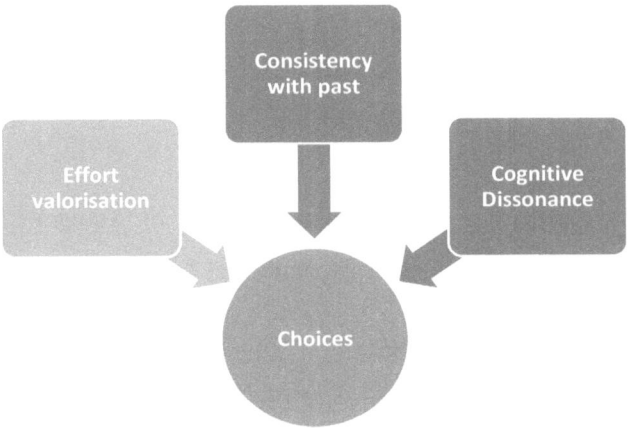

To recapitulate, the integration of purchasing decisions into the internal narrative of the consumer takes place through a story that we tell ourselves (and, sometimes, to others).

This integration can be (and often is) done through the adoption of a story that the brand tells us.

This situation is exemplifying the importance that Storytelling can have in today's marketing.

4.1. Storytelling

What is this, after all, about the storytelling that so many people talk about today and what importance can it have for the success of the startups?

Do you remember Cinderella? Sleeping Beauty? King Arthur?

And remember the report you read at the end of last week?

Because...

Storytelling could be defined as the art of transmitting information that the recipient will remember for a long time.

The difficulty that audiences reveal in retaining and remembering the information transmitted to them results, above all, from the lack of emotional involvement in the transmission of this information.

In other words, people remember a story, especially if it has the key ingredients of the millennial art of storytelling and remembers information that is "embedded" in it.

If this same information is transmitted "dry", people will not remember anything, after 2 minutes.

In addition, a story always draws the attention of the hearer because the human being is genetically programmed to listen and pay attention to stories, the result of thousands of years of evolution in which the transmission of knowledge between generations was done in this way.

Someone begins to tell a story and we pay attention without giving it. We cannot help it.

Instead, someone starts to debit information (for example, with a list of Powerpoint bullets) and we ... hang up, our mind goes away, possibly remember old stories ... We also cannot avoid it.

What are these "key ingredients" that characterize a good story, a good storytelling?

If you remember the children's stories told you as a child, or if you look at Hollywood movies, you will recognize in almost every one of the following elements.

- The story is told following a plot with some fundamental stages;

- There is a conflict between good and evil, the result of which is difficult to predict. It is uncertain whether it will end well or not.

The steps of a good story are easy to identify in any fairy story:

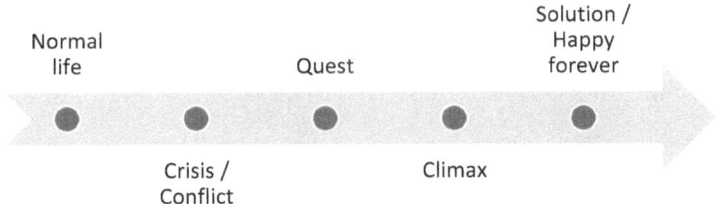

There is an initial phase in which all is well and then a crisis arises, an event that puts everything in question, making it clear that a conflict has arisen between evil (usually very strong) and good (usually less strong and seemingly disadvantaged). It's the stepmother who marries Cinderella's father, or the witch who takes Sleeping Beauty to prick her finger on the loom...

From there we enter the quest phase, a journey, a quest to solve the crisis and conquer the conflict, usually with several twists. It's the learning that Luke Skywalker needs to do with Yoda or the protection of the 7 dwarves to Snow White...

Until this "journey / quest" culminates in the moment of truth, at the climax. It is at this time that the good conquers the conflict with evil and we become a situation of "happily ever after". It is here that Darth Vader turns against the emperor or that Beauty falls in love with the Beast, even before the last petal of the rose falls...

In some "dark" movies ... no! Conflict is not overcome by good!

This aspect of the conflict is essential to capture the attention of the audience. The uncertainty in the outcome, the curiosity to see how the good will overcome the difficulties and disadvantages trap the spectator to the cinema bench (or sofa at home) and create an emotional connection with the hero of the story that leads the viewer to "feel" the same emotions as him. These emotions will be responsible for the recording in the memory of the viewer of the information that was transmitted. Remember, for example, that this is how Hollywood movies took their cigarettes all over the world.

To integrate storytelling into marketing strategy, we need to remember that the consumer goes through the process we call the rationalization of their choices, creating an internal narrative composed of several stories / narratives for the different areas of their life.

To help him change his habits or, on the contrary, to maintain them, we can bring him stories that he can integrate into his inner narrative, preferably stories of heroes he can revise, with whom he can to connect.

Brand image, brand communication, should be done in a way that shows the consumer a better story than his current narrative, so he wants to change (or maintain).

That is, the brand must build a superiority perception (everything that counts for the consumer's decision), showing the consumer how their current narrative can be improved. Let's show the consumer stories he wants to adopt, because they are better than his current narrative.

Of course it helps a lot if the new product is actually better than the existing ones, but that's not enough. It is necessary to show the consumer a history of using the new product in which the hero is clearly better than his current narrative.

Analyzing consumer needs and satisfaction thus essentially involves understanding the story that he tells himself (and some other people) today. From there we will know how we can show you a better story.

From there we can:

1. Choose the content of the story that we are going to target for each target segment (we'll get back to this);

2. Draw stories for each target segment, according to the best storytelling principles we saw above (these are the stories that will create "tribes" of consumers);

3. Give these stories the most appropriate way for the chosen channels of communication (video, books, articles, written ads, sound announcements, ...)

In current marketing we will microsegment the market, which could mean a multitude of different messages / stories, but that is for another section later.

4.2. Create consumption habits

> Habit: automatic behavior triggered by situational suggestions.

A startup, in order to compete on an equal footing with the incumbents, must do everything to create habits of consumption, leading the consumer to change their old habits, using the same psychological mechanisms that the most advanced have been employing.

The best way to do this is to adopt and follow the Hook model[3].

This model assumes that it is only possible to create habits for behaviors that are sufficiently frequent and whose utility is perceived by the consumer as sufficiently important.

It basically consists of a 4-stage cycle which, if repeated a sufficient number of times, gives rise to a new habit. The model is actually intended to link the consumer problem to a solution (our product / service), with the frequency necessary to create a habit. From there, the consumer gets "accustomed" to solve that problem / need with that product / service (ours).

---

[3] Eyal, Nir (2014) **Hooked: How to Build Habit-Forming Products**. Penguim, NYC

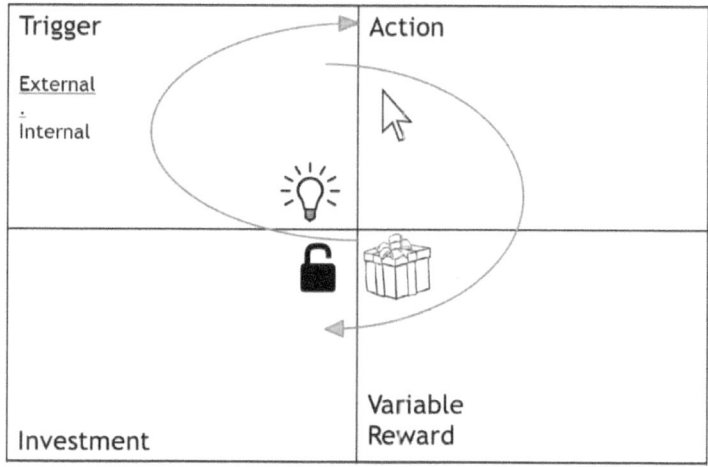

In a simple and somewhat simplistic way, we can say that all behaviors are triggered by something, a trigger, which can be internal or external. This trigger takes the person to take a certain action, which allows him to receive a certain reward. Finally, the product / service must provide some form of investment that will lead the consumer to want to return and want to repeat the whole cycle.

Typically, behaviors are triggered by a factor that reminds the consumer of the need to resolve a situation (take the example of a crisis situation where toilet paper is missing there).

These triggers can be internal or external. The former manifest automatically in the mind, while the latter are produced by the environment and stimulate the senses of the person.

When we are launching a new product / service, there are no internal triggers that lead the consumer to look for it because there is still no connection between our solution (product / service) and the problem that the consumer needs to solve.

We then need to start by using external triggers. If we succeed in the future this will no longer be necessary.

What external triggers (stimulates the senses) can we use:

- Payments (i.e. advertising, whether on or offline);

- Acquired (that is, typically the result of public relations, such as articles or videos / viral posts on social networks or the actual placement in the app store);

- Relational (like likes and comments on social networks, word of mouth advertising, ...);

- Own (occupy a space in the user's environment, such as the apps icons on the phones).

Through one or several of these external Triggers we remind the consumer that the toilet paper in the home may be exhausted, so that it goes to the next phase: action.

As we have seen, there are also internal Triggers that can have the same effect. In fact, we want these internal Triggers in the future to lead the consumer to seek our solution. All Triggers do is alert the consumer to the problem, we will want to build a connection between the problem and our solution.

What are the internal triggers (are they automatically manifested in the mind)? Emotions!

- Negative emotions (boredom, loneliness, frustration, confusion, indecision) that create a little pain and it will lead us to some action;
    - In fact, our life is made up of small stressors that cause us to react to resolve them.
- Positive emotions (something rarer).

Are you bored? Go to Facebook to look for posts with dramatic titles.

Are you stressed? Calm down with Pinterest.

Are you lonely? Go to Facebook / Twitter to search for friends.

Uncertainty, are you in doubt? Go to Google to do a search.

Going back to the previous example, what can alert us to the problem of the lack of toilet paper is the fear (negative emotion) of needing to go to the toilet and...

Hardly a positive emotion will remind us of the lack of toilet paper. Will the satisfaction of having a beautiful toilet paper (black) make us think about it and remember the lack?

Easier an advertisement with a cute dog playing with rolls of toilet paper will remind us of this...

Trigger triggered that reminds us of the problem, we take action ... let's solve the problem.

Here, we need to connect the user problem to our solution. His action must be to seek our solution.

What we know is that for the behavior we want to happen it is necessary to meet two conditions: ability and motivation. Capacity and motivation. We need the consumer to be able (and able) to do this behavior and we need him to want to be motivated to do so.

Beginning with ability, we know that at least 6 factors affect the ability of the consumer to perform any behavior:

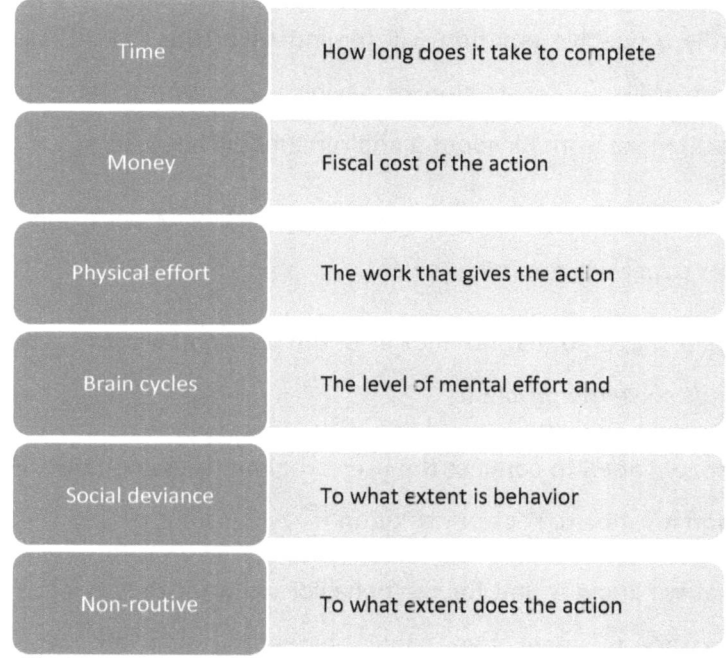

That is, we can say that the longer it takes, the more money it costs, the more physical effort it requires, the more effort and mental focus it requires, the less it is accepted by others and the more it breaks the routine, the more difficult a behavior will be consumer. And vice versa.

We therefore need to do everything to increase the consumer's ability, reducing these obstacles to the maximum, so that the consumer does not stop buying our toilet paper because of lack of money, time, physical or mental laziness, so do not be accepted by society or by putting an end to its routines.

With regard to motivation, what we know about what motivates all human behavior can be summarized as follows:

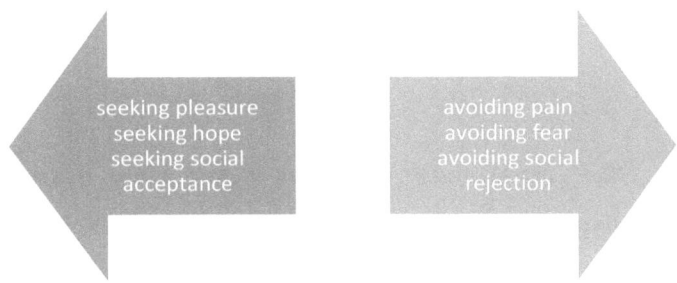

The human being wants pleasure or at least avoid pain.

You want hope or at least avoid fear.

It wants to be accepted socially or at least not be rejected.

Any of them can lead the consumer to take action, the behavior we want, we must choose. Returning to our example, the consumer is afraid of running out of toilet paper and the way to avoid this fear that we want him to adopt is to buy our product.

Once we get the consumer to take the action we wanted, he will have access to his reward. That's why we chose our product / service!

We must take into account that, in fact, the reward that our product / service gives the consumer will fit into at least one of 3 types:

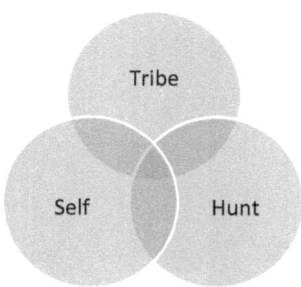

Tribe: Being more accepted, being more attractive, being more important, being more inclusive are social rewards that nurture relationships with other people. In the background, they are gratifications received from others, for using that product / service.

Hunt: the search for material resources (things, money) and information.

Self: People seek to gain a sense of competence, mastery, consistency or completion.

Adding mystery to these rewards makes everything more appealing. The rewards have to align with the narrative we give the consumer so he can use the product and align with the internal consumer motivations and triggers. We must still make these experiences variable, to keep the mystery that makes people want to return. Otherwise, people will end up feeling dissatisfied and "wanting more", making room for them to adhere to the narratives of competitors. This is what explains *the success of the many varieties of toilet paper, with many colors, many designs, recycled, double-leaf, ... in a product that has a supposedly extremely simple function, right?*

We have reached the final phase of the Hook model, in which the stakes are the anticipation of future rewards and no longer obtaining immediate rewards.

We know that the more consumers invest in our brand, the more difficulty it will take to change. That's why people hardly exchange Facebook or LinkedIn for other social networks: they've invested years of their lives in those products, abandoning this investment is very difficult.

We also know, as we have seen previously, that consumer choices are greatly conditioned by the past:

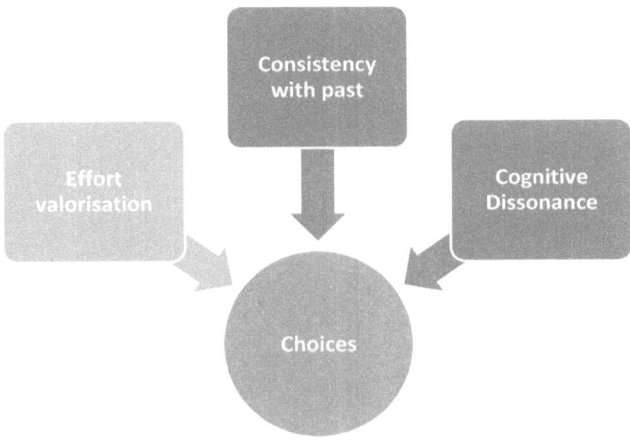

Armed with this knowledge of the psychology of the formation of consumption habits, startups are more likely to achieve a success that can only go through changing the current consumption habits of consumers.

4.3. Psychometrics

It will be easier to achieve this goal if we use the profound knowledge that psychology has offered us for decades on the psychological profile of the consumer, with the so-called OCEAN model, which evaluates human beings based on 5 personality traits.

This model is extraordinarily accurate in assessing people's needs and fears and predicting people's behavior, but has not been used in the past by marketing because of the difficulty in collecting data, which had to be done through a complicated and highly personal questionnaire.

The model evaluates 5 characteristics of personality of the people.

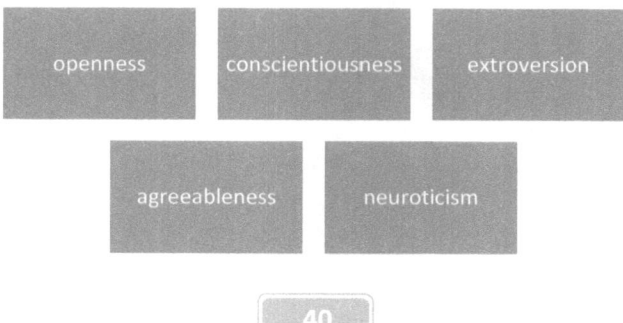

Based on these 5 dimensions, we can make a fairly accurate assessment of each person.

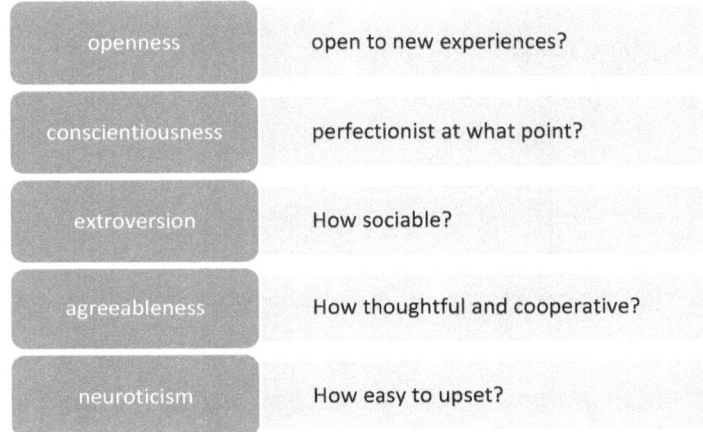

If until recently this model, despite its robustness and predictability ability was not used because of the difficulty in collecting data, today this is no longer a problem thanks to the sea of data that we all started to produce daily consciously and unconsciously.

In fact, several studies have demonstrated the ease of using the information left on social networks to apply the OCEAN model and to evaluate the personality of the people.

Based only on Facebook's likes, you can predict with incredible accuracy the behavior of people. It is unbelievable that:

- With 70 likes we know more than friends of the person;

- With 150, more than parents;

- With 300, more than the spouse.[4]

It is easy (and scary) to verify that with sufficient information we can predict the behaviors of the person better and before her own.

4.4. Big Data Marketing

A startup can overcome its initial disadvantage by using the same technologies as the more advanced incumbents. You can use consumer data stacks, which he (and all of us) leave everywhere, especially on social networks (likes, photos, number of photos, number of friends, geolocation, microsegment the market based on psychometric variables).

We have previously seen that the consumer works on the basis of buying habits, and we have seen that he rationalizes these habits with an internal narrative, telling stories to himself.

The idea is to study these stories and cross them with the psychometric profile of the consumer, the aforementioned OCEAN model.

---

[4] http://applymagicsauce.com/

After that we can use multi-segment and micro-directed messages to "show a better story" to the consumer and create new consumption habits, using the Hook model.

4.5. Microtargeted communication

This aspect of communication was purposely left to the end because it is the sexiest side of marketing but if it is not integrated into a coherent strategy and uses the latest marketing technologies, it will be doomed to failure.

The communication has undergone several transformations in the most recent times that we can summarize in 3 phases:

1. Preacher model

The "preacher" model prevailing since the beginning of time (for example in medieval fairs) to web 1.0 consisted of a salesperson shouting (at first, literally) for their customers a message that was supposed to persuade them to buy their product / service.

2. Network model

The preacher model was replaced when the consumer became a consumer-producer of information, when the brands ceased to dominate communication and could only try to listen and influence what is said about them. This happened essentially with the advent of social networks, or web 2.0.

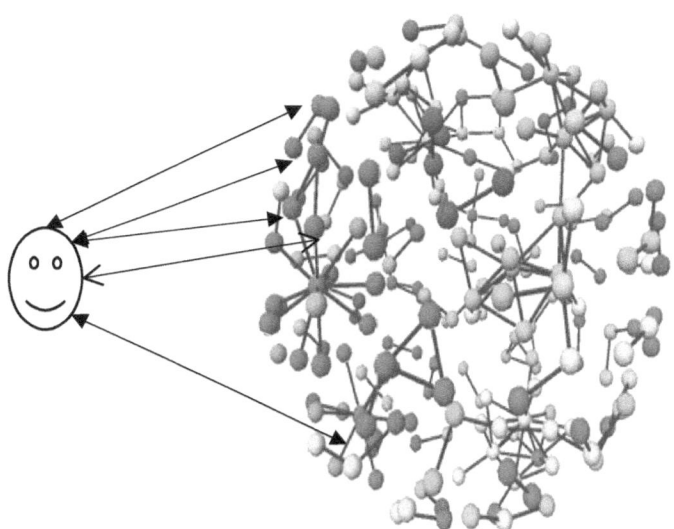

3. Multidirected communication model

Rather than attempting to influence non-controlling communication, brands today can regain control of communication with numerous sources (robots) by sending micro-messages to micro-segments, if necessary by multiplying those sources to make independent communications irrelevant.

That is, segmenting the market into microsegments, based on psychometric variables, evaluated using Big Data methods to analyze the ocean of data made available by the consumer today, we can address each microsegment a specific message using it (if necessary) bots.

This means that the brand regains control of the communication.

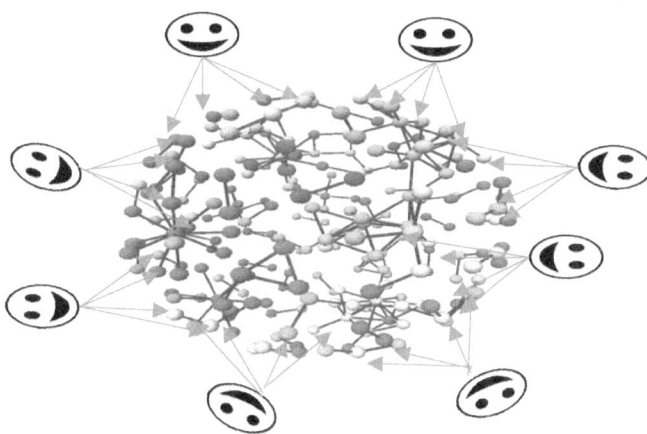

It also means that the brand can abandon the concept, central to the marketing technology of the past, of unique positioning.

The Unique Selling Proposition (USP), the unique (and clear and simple) positioning was an absolutely central concept in marketing and was an undisputed concept. Nobody objected, because if you could pass a USP to the consumer, it was already difficult, imagine what it would be like to try to pass on several ideas.

This is precisely what multidirectional communication allows. One positioning for each microsegment. A different benefit of the product / service highlighted for each different segment.

Marketing technology of the 21st century.

Ferrari!

Want to compete with your bike, which was invented in the 19th century?

5. Conclusions

In fact, we are not proposing that you bring your own Ferrari to this race, because if you are creating a startup I doubt the budget will be enough...

In fact, this marketing technology of the 21st century is characterized by a much higher degree of effectiveness, which allows us to get the right message to the right micro-segment, and only to that. No redundancy (redundancy was the key word of marketing in the time when it made up for making an ad following the evening newspaper of the only television channel).

While it is true that most startups fail because of sales, it is also true that this can be greatly improved if startup devotes as much attention to marketing technology as it devotes to product technology.

That is, if you do not want to compete against the Ferraris of the competition with a bike, even if it is a carbon fiber bike, special race!

If you compete with a Tesla or other electric sports car, you will have a better chance of success. And the budget for fuel will be much smaller. The initial investment is actually done in study and knowledge, so it does not depend so much on the budget.

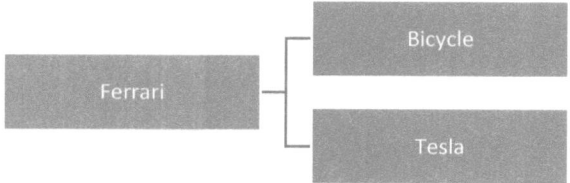

Choosing the Tesla instead of the bike is within the reach of the startups thanks to the technologies of marketing of the XXI century, previously described and that we can combine in a graph like this one:

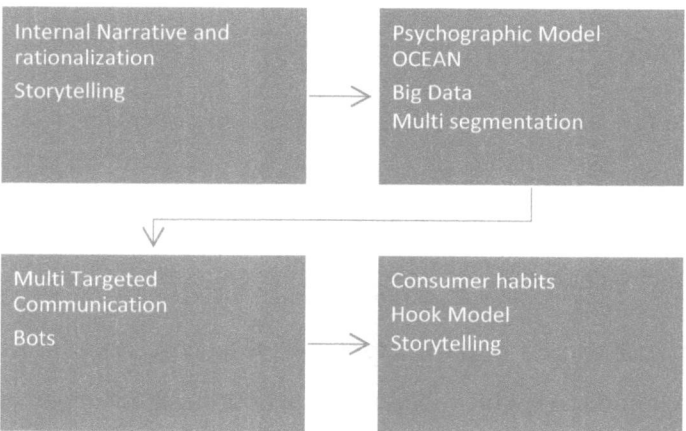

In the end, it is possible to give a much brighter fate to the new (and often fantastic) products / services that are developed by startups combining 3 elements: the behavioral model (psychometric) OCEAN, Big Data and microdirected communication.

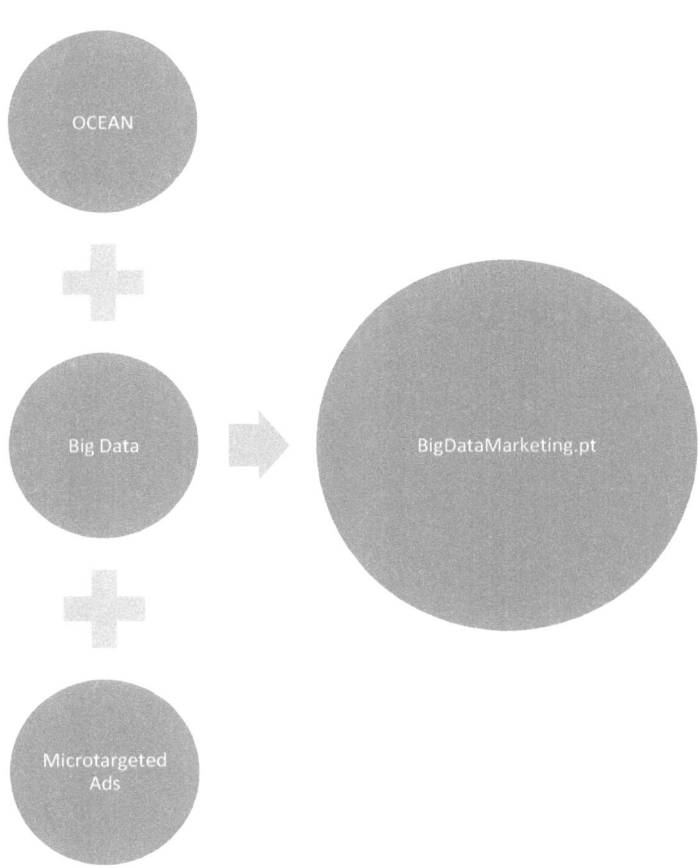

The next invention of Sophia and Lara will not stop at the hands of a German multinational, as it did in the despair of previous experience.

The two young women now know they need to review the habits of doctors and insurance companies and set up a micro-directed communication campaign to show each microsegment a better story, demonstrating that they can improve the lives of their patients and clients by using the new product they are develop. Unfortunately, for commercial reasons they did not want to say what it is yet. They want their stories to be amazing…. and surprising!

6. Bio note

Fernando C. Gaspar (1963). PhD in Management on entrepreneurship, at the Lusíada University of Lisbon. Degree in economics and MBA at Universidade Nova de Lisboa.

Assistant Professor at the Polytechnic Institute of Santarém where he teaches Marketing and Entrepreneurship.

Foto: Mário Aguiam   fernando.gaspar@esg.ipsantarem.pt

Papers and communications published in three languages at national and international scientific conferences and journals and available here.

Published books:

- Gestão de Empresas (1993) ISEGI, Lisboa. ISBN: 972-8093-04-7.
- O Processo Empreendedor e a Criação de Empresas de Sucesso (2009) Edições Sílabo, Lisboa. ISBN 978-972-618-525-3
- O Comércio de Sucesso e a Distribuição no Novo Milénio (2011) Edições Bubok, Spain, ISBN 978-989-97016-0-1
- Dicionário de Gestão (2014) Escolar Editora, Lisboa. ISBN: 9789725924358
- Porque Falham as Startups? E o que podemos aprender com isso? (2017) Amazon, NY. ISBN: 9781549677526

Founding Member of AUDAX - Center for Research and Support to Entrepreneurship and Family Business (ISCTE).

He was President and creator of the Delegation in Santarém of the National Association of Young Entrepreneurs (ANJE), technical director of European projects INTERREG MED and member of the management of SNESup - National Union of Higher Education.

He was himself an entrepreneur, having created companies in the software, real estate and consulting sectors and acquired others in the paint and plastics industries. He also created sports clubs, cultural associations and new activities within the companies he went through.

Since 2012, he has been the director of the Promoting Association of the Dynamic XXI Network (APREDIN), which groups municipalities, technology parks, universities and individuals interested in promoting economic development through innovation and entrepreneurship. fernando.gaspar@apredin.com.pt

He was vice-president of the organizing committee of the General States of Management in the Countries of Latin Expression (EGGPEL) in 2012 and vice-president of the organizing committee of the Congress of Entrepreneurship and Innovation in Latin American Countries (CEIPEL) in 2018.

It was through APREDIN technical coordinator of the INTERREG MED Technopolis project (2007-2013) that it developed a network of technological interface structures and developed training courses in 7 regions of 5 countries of Mediterranean Europe (Portugal, Spain,

France, Italy and Greece). Prior to that, he participated in the INTERREG MEDDOC Technopolis project (2003-2006) and currently in the project INTERREG MED 4helix+.

www.fernando-gaspar.com
www.rededinamicaxxi.pt
fernando.gaspar@apredin.com.pt

www.ingramcontent.com/pod-product-compliance
Lightning Source LLC
Chambersburg PA
CBHW031531210526
45463CB00010B/2812